American Symbols
AND THEIR Meanings

THE
WHITE
HOUSE

American Symbols AND THEIR Meanings

THE
WHITE
HOUSE

HAL MARCOVITZ

MASON CREST PUBLISHERS
PHILADELPHIA

Produced by OTTN Publishing, Stockton, N.J.

Mason Crest Publishers
370 Reed Road
Broomall PA 19008
www.masoncrest.com

3 5 7 9 8 6 4 2

Library of Congress Cataloging-in-Publication Data

Marcovitz, Hal.
  The White House / Hal Marcovitz.
      p. cm. — (American symbols and their meanings)
Summary: The history of the White House, including the story of its constructon, interesting and important facts and statistics, and its importance as an American symbol.
  Includes bibliographical references and index.
  ISBN 1-59084-024-0
1. White House (Washington, D.C.)—Juvenile literature.
2. White House (Washington, D.C.)—History—Juvenile literature.
3. Presidents—United States—History—Juvenile literature.
4. Washington (D.C.)—Buildings, structures, etc.—Juvenile literature. [1. White House (Washington, D.C.)]
I. Title. II. Series.
F204.W5 M27 2003
975.3—dc21
                                            2002009589

Publisher's note: all quotations in this book come from original sources, and contain the spelling and grammatical inconsistencies of the original text.

American Symbols AND THEIR Meanings

CONTENTS

The Importance of American Symbols

Symbols are not merely ornaments to admire—they also tell us stories. If you look at one of them closely, you may want to find out why it was made and what it truly means. If you ask people who live in the society in which the symbol exists, you will learn some things. But by studying the people who created that symbol and the reasons why they made it, you will understand the deepest meanings of that symbol.

The United States owes its identity to great events in history, and the most remarkable American Symbols are rooted in these events. The struggle for independence from Great Britain gave America the Declaration of Independence, the Liberty Bell, the American flag, and other images of freedom. The War of 1812 gave the young country a song dedicated to the flag, "The Star-Spangled Banner," which became our national anthem. Nature gave the country its national animal, the bald eagle. These symbols established the identity of the new nation, and set it apart from the nations of the Old World.

To be emotionally moving, a symbol must strike people with a sense of power and unity. But it often takes a long time for a new symbol to be accepted by all the people, especially if there are older symbols that have gradually lost popularity. For example, the image of Uncle Sam has replaced Brother Jonathan, an earlier representation of the national will, while the Statue of Liberty has replaced Columbia, a woman who represented liberty to Americans in the early 19th century. Since then, Uncle Sam and the Statue of Liberty have endured and have become cherished icons of America.

Of all the symbols, the Statue of Liberty has perhaps the most curious story, for unlike other symbols, Americans did not create her. She was created by the French, who then gave her to America. Hence, she represented not what Americans thought of their country but rather what the French thought of America. It was many years before Americans decided to accept this French goddess of Liberty as a symbol for the United States and its special role among the nations: to spread freedom and enlighten the world.

This series of books is valuable because it presents the story of each of America's great symbols in a freshly written way and will contribute to the students' knowledge and awareness of them. It it to be hoped that this information will awaken an abiding interest in American history, as well as in the meanings of American symbols.

—*Barry Moreno,*
librarian and historian
Ellis Island/Statue of Liberty National Monument

The Executive Mansion, the residence of the president of the United States, is destroyed by British troops who were raiding Washington, D.C., during the War of 1812. Although the soldiers set fire to the building, gutting the rooms inside, the stone walls remained standing. The mansion was rebuilt after the war, and eventually received the nickname by which it has become known: the White House.

PERILOUS MOMENTS

*D*olley Madison was the first First Lady to understand that the White House should be more than just a place for the *president* and his family to reside in Washington while the president served his term in office. The White House, she believed, should be a symbol of America, a place where the styles and tastes of the young country could be displayed to the world.

And so she set about furnishing and decorating the White House with taste and grand style. For help she called on the talents of Benjamin Henry Latrobe. Latrobe was the official *architect* of the federal government, responsible for overseeing many of the construction projects in the nation's *capital*. One of his main responsibilities was construction of the United States *Capitol*, the building where *Congress* would meet to decide the nation's business.

Latrobe agreed to take time off from his official duties to help Mrs. Madison decorate the Executive Mansion. As he decorated the rooms, he asked Mrs. Madison's opinion. "I consider it my duty to follow her directions in all things relative to the President's House," he wrote.

Benjamin Henry Latrobe was born and educated in England, but as a young man learning civil engineering and architecture in the late 18th century, he traveled extensively in Italy and was influenced by the buildings he found there. Years later, after President Thomas Jefferson appointed him "Surveyor of Public Buildings" in Washington, he supervised the construction of many of the young nation's first government buildings. That is a reason many federal buildings in Washington are based on the Roman and Greek styles of architecture.

Latrobe was born in 1764 in Yorkshire, England. He was a hard-working architect, responsible for a number of projects, including the renovation of most of London's police stations. Following the death of his wife in 1795, Latrobe moved to America, where he owned land. He spent the next 10 years designing comfortable homes for wealthy Americans as well as a variety of other structures, such as a prison in Virginia and a bank in Philadelphia. In 1803, Jefferson placed him in charge of the government's vast building program.

Latrobe died of yellow fever in 1820 while supervising the construction of the New Orleans water supply system in Louisiana.

Dolley Madison felt that the Executive Mansion should be the center of Washington society, a place where the president would meet and entertain visiting dignitaries from foreign nations, and where parties would be held celebrating important national events. Washington Irving, the American author, attended one of Mrs. Madison's parties in 1811. He wrote that Dolley Madison was a "fine, portly, buxom dame who has a smile and pleasant word for everybody."

But as Latrobe and Mrs. Madison concerned themselves with fabrics and furniture, President Madison had more pressing issues on his mind. The British had never fully accepted their defeat at the hands of the colonists in the American Revolution. After the war ended in 1783, the British continued fighting with the French, their long-time enemies. Because Great Britain needed sailors for its navy, in 1802 English warships started kidnapping American sailors and pressing them into service. Within a few years, the British began to attack American ships sailing to France. Congress called on American ships to return fire. Finally, on June 18, 1812, President Madison declared war on Britain.

The war did not go well. On August 24, 1814, Mrs. Madison found herself rushing about the Executive

Mansion, hastily packing her family's belongings into crates. A British army was advancing on Washington. The president was safely away from Washington at the time, but Dolley knew she would have to flee the capital or risk capture by the British.

Most of the furnishings in the White House had to be left behind, simply because there was not room in the wagons to save everything. But as Mrs. Madison hurried through her home, she noticed a portrait of George Washington painted by Gilbert Stuart still hanging on a wall. The portrait had been a fixture in the White House since the mansion opened in 1800, and Dolley knew she had to save it. She ordered the portrait cut out of its frame and packed into a wagon.

Later that afternoon, the British soldiers arrived in Washington. They found the White House empty. In fact, the table was still set for a meal. Most of the other government buildings were empty as well.

The aim of the British soldiers was clear: burn the White House to the ground. Louis Barbe Sérurier, the French minister to the United States, saw a detachment of British soldiers with lighted torches heading for the Executive Mansion. Sérurier sent a note to the British commander, General Robert Ross, asking that the White House be spared the torch.

"My messenger found General Ross in the White House, where he was collecting in the drawing room all the furniture and preparing to set it on fire," Sérurier later wrote to Charles Maurice Talleyrand, the French foreign minister. Ross told Sérurier that he would not burn the White House, but that was a lie.

The fire was lit, and the White House burned most of that afternoon. But in the early evening hours, a fierce late-summer thunderstorm swept through Washington. The rains drenched the fire, extinguishing the flames before the White House was destroyed. The fire set by the British soldiers had gutted much of the interior, but the sturdy stone exterior walls of the mansion were mostly undamaged. On the morning following the fire, the White House remained standing.

The American people were horrified that the British would burn down the home of their president. Even the English people questioned their army's conduct in the American capital. "The Cossacks spared Paris, but we spared not the capital of America," wrote the *London Statesman* newspaper.

The Americans and British would eventually agree to peace terms. The White House was rebuilt. President James Monroe and his family became the first occupants of the reconstructed mansion in 1817.

And just as Dolley Madison had envisioned, the White House became more than just a place for America's first family to reside. It would grow into a familiar symbol of the American president, who over the next two centuries would become the most important and powerful person on Earth.

Although George Washington never lived in the White House, his contributions to the design and construction of the mansion should not be overlooked. Washington took a personal interest in construction of the White House during the 1790s.

"THE BEST OF BLESSINGS ON THIS HOUSE"

By 1790, America had won its independence from the British. The Constitution had been written, providing the young nation with a set of laws. General George Washington, the hero of the American Revolution, was elected the first president. New York City was serving as the capital of the United States.

Congress ordered that a new capital city be built on land given to the federal government by the states of Virginia and Maryland. The land was located along the Potomac River. Congress decided the first two buildings erected in the new city would be the Capitol—the place where the Congress would meet and write the nation's

The original layout of Washington, D.C., from a 1793 drawing. The location of the White House is marked by the yellow building near the center of the drawing, which is labeled "President's House." The yellow structure near the top of the map is the U.S. Capitol.

laws—and the President's House, a residence for the government's chief executive. The goal set by Congress for completion of the first two buildings was 1800.

Planning for the Capitol and President's House began under the watchful eye of George Washington, who took a personal interest in the project. He selected a plan for the President's House that had been submitted by James Hoban, an Irish-born architect who based his design on the mansion occupied by the Duke of Leinster in Dublin, Ireland. Hoban's design was for a house that would rise three stories from the ground, feature tall stone columns out front, and include a grand entrance hall and elegant dining rooms. Throughout the building, there would be wide stairways and corridors, high ceilings, and prominent windows.

At the time, there were few houses in America that

could compare to what Hoban envisioned for the President's House. Most Americans of the 1790s were of modest means and few could afford grand homes.

Congress provided $200,000 for construction of the President's House—an amount that would prove insufficient by the time the project was completed. In fact, Hoban would spend $400,000 of the government's money to build the mansion.

Hoban was assigned to direct the work. During the

George Washington wanted the President's House to be as luxurious as the home of any ruler in Europe. Washington wanted the United States to be taken seriously by the European monarchs, and he aimed for them to be impressed with his country's wealth.

Washington read over the plans submitted by several architects who had entered a competition to design the President's House, finally selecting the winner himself.

For the five years he served in office while the mansion was under construction, Washington was very demanding when it came to the project and would often dismiss arguments with a curt, "I require it." Since few people in the federal city dared dispute Washington, when it came to the White House the president usually got what he wanted.

Washington left office in 1797, three years before the President's House was completed. For most of his eight years in office, George and Martha Washington made their home in a rented house on Cherry Street in New York City, which at the time served as the temporary capital of the United States while the District of Columbia was under construction.

seven years the President's House was under construction, Hoban lived in a cottage on the construction grounds. The cornerstone for the White House was laid on October 13, 1792.

James Hoban was paid $500 for designing and supervising construction of the White House. The job lasted seven years.

Hoban found an abundant source of stone for the outer walls in nearby Aquia Creek in Virginia. The stone taken out of the creek bed was sandstone, a tough but very *porous* stone, meaning that it absorbs water during rainstorms. When stone absorbs water it becomes weak. Inside the stone, the water will freeze during the winter. When water freezes, it expands. The constant freezing and thawing of water inside stone will make it brittle and chips will flake off over time. Eventually the stone will crumble. Any building erected with blocks made out of sandstone has to be sealed with a paint that prevents water from entering the stone.

In 1798, as the President's House was nearing completion, Hoban ordered the workers to apply a thick coat of white paint to the exterior walls. He told them to be sure to force the paint into every crack, seam, and joint they found in the massive stone walls.

Soon the President's House had received its first coat of

The original cornerstone for the White House remains buried somewhere on the grounds and has never been found.

During his first few days living in the White House, John Adams wrote, "I pray Heaven to bestow the best of blessings on this house, and on all that shall hereafter inhabit it. May none but honest and wise men ever rule under this roof!" These words would eventually be carved above the mansion's central fireplace.

white paint, covering the dark gray sandstone. As work continued over the next two years, residents of the District of Columbia found themselves referring to the President's House as the "White House." At this time, though, it was nothing more than a nickname for the home of the nation's chief executive.

In November 1800, the second president of the United States, John Adams, and his wife Abigail moved into the White House. The White House had been built before the deadline set by Congress eight years before. However, few of the mansion's 30 rooms were complete, the main staircase had not yet been built, and no firewood had been gathered for the coming cold winter. Mrs. Adams hardly felt at home. "Not one room or chamber is finished of the whole," she wrote to her sister. "It is habitable by fires in every part, thirteen of which we are obliged to keep daily, or sleep in wet and damp places."

The Adamses didn't stay long. John Adams would lose re-election to Thomas Jefferson, who moved in shortly after his inauguration in March 1801. Work was continuing on the White House as well as many other government buildings in the federal city. Just one wing of the Capitol had been completed. Also underway were buildings housing the Treasury and State Departments as well as buildings that would serve as headquarters for the army and navy.

Even though Jefferson was only the second occupant of the White House, he had many of his own ideas for the residence and insisted on many changes to Hoban's original design. He directed that a fence be built around the entire property. Jefferson also wanted to add places where the president and his staff would work to the White House. The additions would be called the East and West Wings. Work on the wings started in 1805.

Thomas Jefferson, the man who wrote the Declaration of Independence, remains one of the most revered presidents in American history. Jefferson was an architect, and as president he insisted on changes to the White House. Jefferson's ideal home was Monticello, which he built for himself in Charlottesville, Virginia.

Meanwhile, the White House needed furniture, window curtains, and art so that it could truly be an elegant residence for the nation's leader. That job should have fallen to the first lady, but by the time of Jefferson's presidency there had been little opportunity for a first lady to furnish the mansion. Martha Washington had never lived at the White House. Abigail Adams left after four months. Thomas Jefferson was a *widower*.

Jefferson turned to Dolley Madison, the wife of his secretary of state, James Madison. Back in 1792, Congress had set aside $15,000 to furnish the mansion and a lot of it was still unspent. Mrs. Madison was given a free hand to spend whatever she needed to make the White House ready for public receptions. For much of Jefferson's presidency as well as the presidency of her husband—until, of course, the fire of 1814—Dolley Madison served as the official White House hostess. Mrs. Madison planned gala dinners almost nightly in the White House, writing the invitations herself.

By the time her husband had been sworn into office in 1809, most of the building projects in Washington were well underway and no longer needed the direct attention of the president, who was by now more concerned with the gathering storm clouds of war with England. Indeed, much of the talk of the coming war was traded by the nation's leaders and the world's diplomats across the dining tables at many of Mrs. Madison's White House parties.

An interior room of the White House, gutted during a major renovation of the building in the early 1950s. The Executive Mansion has been modified many times over the years, with rooms added or expanded to suit the needs of the president and his staff.

A CENTURY OF CHANGE

The President's House earned the nickname "White House" while it was still under construction in the 1790s. Still, it wasn't until Theodore Roosevelt became president in 1901 that the Executive Mansion earned the official title of "White House." Roosevelt simply had the name engraved on his stationery as his address. And so, a letter from the president was now, officially, a letter from the White House.

Since the fire of 1814, many presidents and their families have occupied the White House. Nearly all of them have had their own ideas of what the White House should be, and they ordered the federal government to make changes that suited them.

James Monroe was the first president to move into the White House following its reconstruction. Monroe and his wife, Elizabeth, moved back into the Executive Mansion in late 1817. Before leaving office eight years later, Monroe ordered construction of the South *Portico*—a round, covered porch on the south side of the mansion. In 1829, during the administration of President Andrew Jackson, the North Portico was added. The North Portico served as a covering for the driveway leading up to the house.

Since formal dinners are regular events in the White House, many flowers are constantly needed to decorate the tables. And so a greenhouse was added onto the White House during the presidency of James Buchanan. Over the years, the greenhouse was rebuilt and enlarged and, eventually, a visitor would find several greenhouses on the White House grounds. When Ulysses S. Grant became president after the Civil War, he turned one of the greenhouses into a *billiard* room. When Grant left office, he took his billiard table with him. The next president, Rutherford B. Hayes, remodeled the billiard room so it could be used for dancing.

President James A. Garfield took office in 1881 and ordered the whole White House redecorated. Garfield was assassinated after just a few months in office. The new president, Chester A. Arthur, directed that Garfield's project continue as planned. In fact, on April

14, 1882, the federal government held an auction of old White House furnishings for sale to the public. "Twenty-four wagon loads of old furniture and junk from the White House were sent off," the *Washington Post* newspaper reported the day after the sale. "Only curiosity and desire to examine the housekeeping of a president could have drawn fully 5,000 people and caused a realization from the auction of such goods of about $3,000."

Among the items sold at the auction were "hair mattresses, maps, chandeliers, four marble mantels, bureaus, bedsteads, two high chairs for children, marble-top tables, leather-covered sofas, ottomans and dining room chairs."

During this era, other changes were made to the White House as well. Advances were being made in plumbing, heating, and lighting, and the White House was made ready for them.

When the Adamses first moved in, fireplaces and coal stoves heated the White House. In 1840, a coal-fired furnace was installed. A fireman was hired to feed and maintain the furnace. He was given a room in the White House and required to be on duty 24 hours a day, seven days a week, although he was given summers off.

Gaslights replaced can-

> **A warehouse in Maryland is used to store furniture, china, pieces of art, and other items that aren't in use in the White House. Currently, more than 20,000 items are in storage.**

dles in the White House in 1848. Gas was fed to the White House from a gas pipeline that was laid along Pennsylvania Avenue from the White House to the Capitol. After several blackouts at the White House, it was found that shop owners on Pennsylvania Avenue had illegally tapped into the line and were stealing gas.

By the time Theodore Roosevelt took office, it was clear something was wrong with the White House. Upstairs, the living quarters were hardly suitable for the Roosevelts—the president and Mrs. Roosevelt had six children and only eight rooms of living space on the third floor. Downstairs, the rooms were showing wear and tear and the floors sagged. The dining room was too small to accommodate large crowds for state dinners. The office space was overcrowded. What's more, the building had been altered so much over the years that it now needed extensive structural improvements.

And so, Roosevelt called on the talents of architect Charles Follen McKim to renovate the White House. On June 28, 1902, Congress appropriated $475,000 for the project. The Roosevelts moved out, and McKim got to work. McKim tore out most of the interior walls, moved rooms around, created new spaces and new entrances, and used some of the new building techniques that were just being introduced at the turn of the last century. One of those techniques was the use of steel *I-beams* to support the upper floors of the White House. Unfortunately, McKim ordered the I-beams positioned

In the late 19th century and early 20th century, Charles Follen McKim (at the left in this photo) was perhaps the nation's most respected architect. Along with his partners William Mead (center) and Stanford White (right), McKim designed some of America's most important buildings, including the Boston Public Library, Madison Square Garden

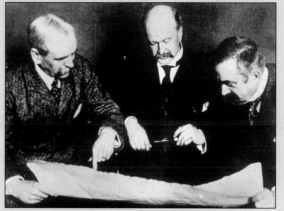

and Pennsylvania Railroad Station in New York, and Agricultural Palace in Chicago. When President Theodore Roosevelt decided the White House needed a top-to-bottom renovation in 1902, he turned to McKim.

McKim immersed himself in the White House project, concluding that the aging mansion needed to be completely gutted and rebuilt. "It is useless to secure a harmonious structure by doing over any one part of the house," he wrote. "If the work is to be done at all, the entire house should be treated as a single problem."

After the White House renovation, McKim, Mead and White grew into the largest and most influential architectural firm in America, with more than 100 employees. The firm set standards for training and conduct of architects that influenced their industry for decades.

over old clay bricks that had been laid during the original construction in the 1790s. They weren't strong enough to support the weight of the steel beams.

In 1948, during the presidency of Harry S. Truman, visitors to the White House couldn't help but notice the

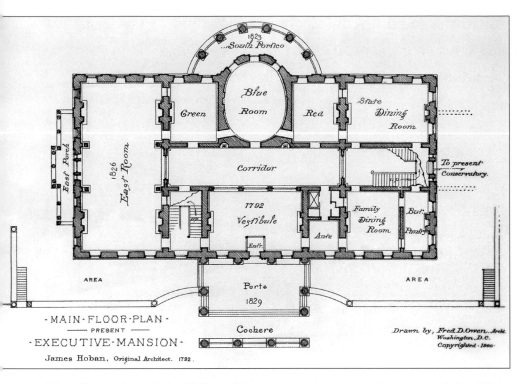

This floor plan of the White House was drawn at the start of the 20th century, to be used by architects on a renovation project around that time. Areas that were added on to the original building during its first 100 years are marked with the dates, such as the South Portico (1823), East Room (1826), and North Portico (1829).

floors were off-level. The steel I-beams were sinking into the bricks, and they were taking the upper floors of the Executive Mansion with them. Congress authorized a study of the problem, but while the study was underway the leg of a piano in daughter Margaret Truman's room broke through the floor and knocked plaster down from the ceiling below.

Another major renovation of the White House was ordered. On June 23, 1949, Congress once again appropriated money for the renovation of the White House.

This time, the bill would come to more than $5 million, and work commenced that December. Once again, the president's family moved out, and the construction workers moved in.

To offset some of the cost of the Truman renovation, rubble from the construction site was sold to the public as souvenirs. A brick, for example, could be bought for a dollar. An old square nail was sold for 50 cents. Sales of the souvenirs raised about $10,000. It was hardly enough to cover the cost of the project, but the public aimed to show its support for the renovation, and the souvenirs sold quickly.

During the renovation, the interior of the White House was completely gutted, leaving only the exterior walls standing. The architects had designed a new basement for the White House that would house many offices as well as storage areas and a bomb shelter. To dig the basement, the engineers proposed that part of an exterior wall be knocked down so that a bulldozer could be driven inside the mansion.

When the idea was brought to President Truman, he immediately said no.

The engineers had no other choice than to have the bulldozer taken apart and carried inside the front door of the White House, piece by piece.

The walls of the White House had not tumbled during James Madison's presidency, nor would they tumble during Harry Truman's presidency.

James Hoban, the architect who designed the White House, was born in 1762 in Kilkenny, Ireland. After studying at the University of Dublin, he moved to America in 1785. In addition to designing the building, Hoban made a decision that would forever affect its appearance: he ordered it painted white.

A LIVING MUSEUM OF AMERICA

The White House has been repainted many times over the years. In 1990, workers stripped the White House down to bare stone and found that it had received 42 coats of paint over the years. Whenever the White House is repainted, it takes 570 gallons of paint to cover the exterior surface.

The White House sits on a 16-acre parcel of land in Washington, D.C. The building measures 170 feet by 85 feet, and rises 58 feet over the ground. The address of the White House is 1600 Pennsylvania Avenue. Tax records on file in Washington value the property at that address at $315 million, while the building itself is valued at about $25 million.

The White House contains 132 rooms, 99 of which are in the basement. There are 412 doors, 147 windows, 28 fireplaces and 7 staircases in the White House. There are 32 bathrooms in the mansion. There is a dental office and a doctor's office in the White House, as well as a bomb shelter. Visitors will find 40 hallways to negotiate.

The song "Hail to the Chief" was first played in the White House during the presidency of James K. Polk. Prior to Polk's administration, the president always greeted guests as they entered a reception hall, usually the East Room. But Polk, who was a bit on the short side, was uncomfortable greeting guests as they entered the room. First Lady Sarah Polk suggested that her husband enter the room accompanied by music after the guests were assembled. She selected the music and accompanied him on his arm as the Marine Band played "Hail to the Chief." The song was from the play "Lady of the Lake," and it had long been one of Mrs. Polk's favorite musical compositions.

Julia Grant was probably the first wife of a president to be referred to as a "First Lady." The term appeared in an 1870 newspaper column written by *journalist*

> President James Monroe, who was the first president to occupy the White House after it was rebuilt following the 1814 fire, kept a fire engine in the White House basement—just in case one would be needed in the future. President John Quincy Adams kept a rowboat in the basement.

President Grover Cleveland is the only president to have been married in the White House. He exchanged vows with Frances Folsom in 1886. Afterward, the president and his wife elected not to live in the White House; they lived instead in a nearby home known as "Red Top," because Cleveland believed the White House lacked privacy.

Emily Briggs. However, Varina Davis, wife of Jefferson Davis, the president of the Confederate States of America during the Civil War, was often referred to as the "First Lady of the Confederacy." Martha Washington was known as Lady Washington. Over the years, other presidents' wives were known as "Mrs. President" or "Presidentress." Jacqueline Kennedy, wife of President John Kennedy, prohibited her staff from referring to her as the First Lady. She assigned an aide to come up with a new title for the wife of the president, but the idea was eventually dropped.

The first telephone was installed in the White House in 1878 during the administration of President Rutherford B. Hayes, who insisted on answering the phone himself. The first phone number for the White

House was "1." Electric lights were installed in 1891, during the presidency of Benjamin Harrison. The first flush toilets were installed in the White House during the administration of President Theodore Roosevelt. The first refrigerator was installed in 1945.

Each first lady is given an opportunity to replace the White House china, the dinnerware used for banquets and receptions. The record for spending on White House china is held by President Ronald Reagan's wife, Nancy, who spent $240,000 on new china. When an outdoor swimming pool was built on the White House grounds in 1975, construction workers unearthed broken pieces of china. Historians concluded the pieces were from Dolley Madison's china set, destroyed in the 1814 fire.

The president and members of his family are protected by the U.S. Secret Service. A special room at the gatehouse of the northwest entrance of the White House is used exclusively by the Secret Service to interview people who try to climb over the fence around the building. About 25 people a year try to break onto the mansion's grounds. Another 4,000 people a year call up the White House and make threats against the president.

People who visit the White House have to pass through strict security measures. In fact, about a dozen people a year try to bring guns into the White House and are caught by metal detectors. They face arrest under a city law in the District of Columbia that prohibits guns in the White House.

The U.S. Army, Navy, Air Force and Marines all provide services at the White House. The army maintains the fleet of limousines and black sedans used in presidential motorcades. The army also provides the operators for the White House switchboard. The navy runs the White House kitchen, although it employs civilian chefs to prepare the president's meals. The Marine Corps supplies the helicopters that lift off from the White House lawn. And the Air Force supplies the pilots for Air Force One, the president's plane.

The White House is more than just a place where the president lives and works; it is also a living museum of America. More than one million people a year tour the White House, although few of the mansion's rooms are open to the public. Another 40,000 people are invited for presidential receptions, parties, dinners, bill-signings and other events.

People who visit the White House have a chance to buy souvenirs. In fact, the White House Souvenir Shop is located in Room 68 in the basement. White House T-shirts are for sale in the store.

The Oval Office, where the president of the United States works, has been called the most powerful office in the world. The office was added to the White House building in 1909.

NEAR THE PRESIDENT'S DOOR

During a remodeling of the West Wing of the White House in 1909, President William Howard Taft was provided with a new office that was called the Oval Office because of its shape. Today, the term "Oval Office" has become so familiar to Americans that whenever a newscaster reports a story about a new development in the Oval Office, all his listeners are immediately aware he is talking about the president.

In 1961, a garden was planted just outside the Oval Office. Roses were mostly planted in the garden and, today, in spring and summer, they bloom in bright colors. The Rose Garden has become one of the most

The White House is a place where festive occasions are celebrated. (Top) Before Christmas, an enormous tree is displayed after an annual White House ceremony. (Right) This turkey strolling the grounds of the White House on Thanksgiving has something to worry about; fortunately, the president usually grants a pardon to the bird.

picturesque and familiar places on the White House grounds. Presidents frequently stage ceremonies there to take advantage of the lively colors. A new law signed by the president in a Rose Garden ceremony is always given coverage on the network newscasts.

The White House is responsible for many other images familiar to the nation. Each winter, the president and first lady light the White House Christmas tree after it has been decorated with orna

> The oak trees on the White House grounds were planted by President John Quincy Adams. He personally hunted for acorns around Washington to plant outside the Executive Mansion.

ments donated from all over the country. In the spring, hundreds of children flock to the grounds at 1600 Pennsylvania Avenue to participate in the annual White House Easter egg hunt.

Each day, a visitor to Washington who stops off in Lafayette Park will likely see dozens of protesters carrying signs or making speeches on any number of topics. That is their right. In America, the Constitution guarantees freedom of speech. They have the right to speak their minds anywhere in America, but many protesters choose Lafayette Park for one reason: the president lives across the street.

While it may be a stretch of the imagination to think the president is listening to every word said in Lafayette Park—the Oval Office is, in fact, located on the opposite side of the mansion—it is nevertheless important to the protesters to carry their message as near the president's door as they can.

Certainly, they aren't allowed on the White House grounds. Security at the White House is tight, and Secret

Service agents are sworn to protect the president with their lives. But they are allowed as close as Lafayette Park, which is just a few hundred feet away from the president's front door.

The act of staging protests in front of the White House probably had its birth on January 10, 1917, when hundreds of women calling for suffrage, the right to vote, marched up and down Pennsylvania Avenue. "How long must women wait for liberty?" asked one of the signs carried by a protester.

The newspapers of the era frowned on protests in front of the White House. "If everyone who wanted some particular measure or legislation undertook to *picket* the White House, it would be besieged by a mob reaching from Baltimore to Washington," wrote the *New York World* newspaper. Nevertheless, in this case, the president was probably paying attention. Women were granted the right to vote three years later.

In January 1991, thousands of people gathered in Lafayette Park to protest the start of the Persian Gulf War. "I thought if the president could see people saying no, it might make him stop," said Beth Aroot, of McLean, Virginia, who had waited in the rain for hours to deliver her message.

> **Among the recreational facilities located on the White House grounds are a jogging track, outdoor swimming pool, one-lane bowling alley, movie theater, artificial golf putting green, basketball court, tennis court, and horseshoe pit.**

Arthur Ashe, a former tennis star and activist, is arrested at a rally in Lafayette Park across the street from the White House. Many protests are conducted in the park. Ashe was protesting U.S. policy on refugees from Haiti in September 1992.

In this case, as well, the president was listening. Although President George Bush elected to go ahead with the war, he later complained that the shouts and drum-beating originating in Lafayette Park were so loud and constant that he lost several nights' sleep.

And so, to the people who express their freedom of speech in Lafayette Park and to those who sit at home and watch the news coverage of the protests on TV or read about them in their newspapers, the White House is a symbol of power. Inside its 200-year-old walls, decisions are made that affect the lives of all Americans and, very often, the lives of everyone on Earth.

1790 The U.S. Congress orders a federal city built on land donated by Virginia and Maryland. The new city will be called the District of Columbia, and its first two buildings will be the Capitol and President's House.

1792 Work begins on the President's House on October 13.

1798 While under construction, the President's House receives its first coat of paint, and soon becomes known to neighbors as the White House.

1800 John and Abigail Adams become the first residents of the White House on November 1.

1805 Work begins on the East and West Wings.

1814 On August 24, British soldiers set fire to the White House; a drenching rain extinguishes the blaze before the exterior walls collapse.

1817 President James Monroe and his wife Elizabeth move into the rebuilt White House.

1824 President Monroe begins construction of the South Portico

1829 The North Portico is constructed.

1833 The first water pipes are installed in the White House.

1848 Gas lighting is installed in the White House.

1881 An elevator is installed in the White House.

1886 President Grover Cleveland marries Frances Folsom in a White House ceremony.

1891 The White House is wired for electricity.

1901 President Theodore Roosevelt adds the term "White House" to his stationery, making the term the official address of the president.

1902 Architect Charles Follen McKim supervises an extensive renovation of the White House.

1909 The Oval Office is added to the West Wing.

1933 A swimming pool is built in the White House; it is paid for with voluntary contributions to President Franklin D. Roosevelt.

1948 A balcony is added to the South Portico

1949 A second major renovation of the White House commences during the presidency of Harry S. Truman.

1961 The Rose Garden is planted on the White House lawn.

2001 An average of 6,000 people visit the White House each day.

architect—designer of buildings.

billiards—game played on a flat table by driving balls into pockets with a long stick, known as a cue.

capital—city that serves as the official center of a nation's government.

Capitol—building in Washington where Congress passes laws and conducts other business.

Congress—legislative branch of the government of the United States, consisting of the House of Representatives and the Senate.

I-beam—metal post that supports a building; when viewed from the end, the post resembles the capital letter "I."

journalist—person who gathers and reports news.

picket—person who joins others in a line of protest in public.

portico—roof supported by columns, usually extending out from a building.

porous—physical characteristics of an object that allows water to enter.

president—chief executive of a country whose authority to govern is provided by popular vote.

widower—man who has lost his wife by death and has not remarried.

FURTHER READING

Caroli, Betty Boyd. *First Ladies*. New York: Oxford University Press. 1995.

Clinton, Hillary Rodham. *An Invitation to the White House*. New York: Simon and Schuster, 2000.

Freidel, Frank, and Pencak, William. *The White House: The First Two Hundred Years*. Boston: Northeastern University Press. 1994.

Karr, Kathleen. *It Happened at the White House: Extraordinary Tales from America's Most Famous House*. New York: Disney Press, 1999.

Seale, William. *The White House: History of an American Idea*. Washington: American Institute of Architects Press. 1992.

INTERNET RESOURCES

Information about the White House

www.nps.gov/whho/
www.whitehouse.gov
www.whitehousehistory.org

Tour of the White House

www.time.com/time/campaign2000/whitehouse/
photo_01.html

PICTURE CREDITS

BARRY MORENO has been librarian and historian at the Ellis Island Immigration Museum and the Statue of Liberty National Monument since 1988. He is the author of *The Statue of Liberty Encyclopedia*, which was published by Simon and Schuster in October 2000. He is a native of Los Angeles, California. After graduation from California State University at Los Angeles, where he earned a degree in history, he joined the National Park Service as a seasonal park ranger at the Statue of Liberty; he eventually became the monument's librarian. In his spare time, Barry enjoys reading, writing, and studying foreign languages and grammar. His biography has been included in *Who's Who Among Hispanic Americans*, *The Directory of National Park Service Historians*, *Who's Who in America*, and *The Directory of American Scholars*.

HAL MARCOVITZ is a journalist for *The Morning Call*, a newspaper based in Allentown, Pennsylvania. He has written more than 20 books for young readers. He lives in Chalfont, Pennsylvania, with his wife, Gail, and their daughters, Ashley and Michelle.